Nutrition

Vitamins

by Janet Slingerland

I0877302

FOCUS READERS

BEACON

www.focusreaders.com

Copyright © 2025 by Focus Readers®, Mendota Heights, MN 55120. All rights reserved. No part of this book may be reproduced or utilized in any form or by any means without written permission from the publisher.

Focus Readers is distributed by North Star Editions:
sales@northstareditions.com | 888-417-0195

Produced for Focus Readers by Red Line Editorial.

Photographs ©: Shutterstock Images, cover, 1, 4, 7, 8, 11, 13, 14–15, 16, 19, 20, 22, 25, 26, 29

Library of Congress Cataloging-in-Publication Data
Names: Slingerland, Janet, author.
Title: Vitamins / by Janet Slingerland.
Description: Mendota Heights, MN: Focus Readers, [2025] | Series: Nutrition | Includes bibliographical references and index. | Audience: Grades 2-3
Identifiers: LCCN 2024001358 (print) | LCCN 2024001359 (ebook) | ISBN 9798889981855 (hardcover) | ISBN 9798889982418 (paperback) | ISBN 9798889983514 (ebook pdf) | ISBN 9798889982975 (hosted ebook)
Subjects: LCSH: Vitamins in human nutrition--Juvenile works. | Vitamins--Juvenile literature.
Classification: LCC QP771 .S575 2025 (print) | LCC QP771 (ebook) | DDC 612.3/99--dc23/eng/20240229
LC record available at https://lccn.loc.gov/2024001358
LC ebook record available at https://lccn.loc.gov/2024001359

Printed in the United States of America
Mankato, MN
082024

About the Author

Janet Slingerland started out studying electrical engineering and programming computers. Now she writes. Janet has authored more than two dozen nonfiction books on a wide variety of topics, including animals and Wi-Fi.

Table of Contents

Chapter 1

Vitamins for Lunch

A girl sits down with her friends at a lunch table. She takes a lunch box out of her backpack. She made the meal last night. It includes several kinds of food.

Packing a healthy lunch can help people get all the vitamins they need.

First, the girl pulls out a wrap. Different foods are rolled up in a whole wheat tortilla. One **ingredient** is a bean filling. Avocado slices add color. Carrots give a bit of crunch.

The wrap has many **nutrients**. The beans have B vitamins. The avocados have vitamin E. And the carrots add vitamin A.

Did You Know?

Many common foods contain several different vitamins.

Cucumbers are good sources of vitamins B and C.

The girl's meal includes even more healthy foods. She nibbles on cucumber slices. Then, she unpeels a tangerine for dessert. The fruit is sweet and tangy. And it's full of vitamin C.

Chapter 2

What Vitamins Do

Vitamins are **organic matter**. That means they come from living things such as plants and animals. The body needs 13 different vitamins. But it only needs tiny amounts of each.

Too much or too little of a vitamin can cause illness.

Vitamins can be sorted into two groups. One type **dissolves** in fat. This group is called fat-soluble vitamins. The human body can store these vitamins.

There are four fat-soluble vitamins. Vitamin A helps with vision. Vitamin D protects bones. Vitamin E protects other vitamins from damage. Vitamin K helps blood stick together.

Water-soluble vitamins are the other type. These vitamins dissolve

Vitamin A is often found in dairy products.

in water. The body cannot store water-soluble vitamins. So, some of these vitamins may not be used. They pass out of the body in urine.

There are nine water-soluble vitamins. Vitamin C is one. It helps keep bones healthy. It also helps the body make collagen. Collagen is a **tissue** that heals wounds.

The other eight water-soluble vitamins are B vitamins. These kinds of vitamins have many uses. They help turn food into energy.

Did You Know?

Vitamin C helps the immune system work properly.

Fruits and vegetables contain large amounts of vitamin C.

They are needed for healthy skin and blood. They also help the brain work properly.

A CLOSER LOOK

Vitamin D

Vitamin D is different from other vitamins. The body makes it. This process starts when sunlight hits the skin. Sunlight changes certain **chemicals** in the skin to vitamin D_3. Vitamin D_3 moves to the liver and kidneys. These **organs** alter the vitamin D_3. It becomes active vitamin D.

Healthy bones need vitamin D. It helps the body take in calcium. Calcium strengthens bone. Without vitamin D, bones can't get enough calcium. They may fracture more easily.

Spending time outside can help people get enough vitamin D.

Chapter 3

Vitamin Sources

Vitamins come from many foods. Some types of food have large amounts of certain vitamins. For example, vitamin A is in many vegetables. Carrots are a good source.

Vitamin A can be found in tomatoes and red bell peppers.

Few foods have vitamin D. Fish has the most. Eggs and cheese have some, too. Some foods have vitamin D added in. Dairy and plant-based milks are common examples. But most of a person's vitamin D is made when sunlight hits the skin.

Vitamin E can be found in many fatty foods. Vegetable oils are good sources of this vitamin. So are nuts and seeds. Almonds and sunflower seeds are two examples. Avocados have lots of vitamin E, too.

Chickpeas are a good source of vitamin K.

Vitamin K is often found in green vegetables. These include spinach and broccoli. Eggs are another good source of vitamin K.

Broccoli and tofu are healthy plant-based sources of B vitamins.

Many sources of vitamin C can be eaten raw. These include oranges and lemons. Strawberries are another example. Vitamin C can also be found in vegetables such as cabbage and cauliflower.

There are eight different B vitamins. Poultry and fish contain lots of these vitamins. Salmon is one healthy source. Eggs and milk are also healthy choices. Leafy greens are another option. These include kale and lettuce.

Did You Know?

Approximately half of a person's daily vitamin K is made by bacteria in the gut.

Chapter 4

Colorful Plates

The body needs all 13 vitamins. So, it is important to eat different kinds of foods each day. Whole foods are best. These are foods that have not been **processed**.

Fresh fruits and vegetables are examples of whole foods.

People should also try to eat foods with different colors. That way, they can get all the vitamins they need. For example, red foods often have lots of vitamin A. Tomatoes are healthy options. Watermelon is a sweeter choice.

Yellow and orange foods have different vitamins. They are often good sources of vitamins C and E. They may also have B vitamins. Carrots and corn are healthy choices. Sweet potatoes are, too.

Green foods often have lots of vitamins A, C, and K.

Green foods are another important group. Leafy greens are one option. Broccoli and peas are also healthy choices.

White and brown foods often provide vitamins C and E. They also have vitamin K.

Purple and blue foods can be good sources of vitamins C and K. Blueberries and blackberries make great snacks.

White and brown foods provide vitamins, too. Cauliflower and onions can be tasty in soups and stir-fries.

Proteins are another important part of a healthy diet. They contain lots of B vitamins. Fish is a healthy source. Tofu is a good plant-based option.

Did You Know?

Some vitamins can be lost when food is cooked in water. People should cook certain vegetables for a short time. That way, the vitamins don't wash out.

FOCUS ON

Vitamins

Write your answers on a separate piece of paper.

1. Write a few sentences describing the main ideas of Chapter 2.

2. What is your favorite source of vitamin C? What do you like about it?

3. Which vitamin helps with vision?

   A. vitamin A

   B. vitamin K

   C. vitamin E

4. What might happen to a person who does not spend much time outside?

   A. She might get too much collagen.

   B. She might not get enough vitamin D.

   C. She might get heart disease.

5. What does **alter** mean in this book?

*Vitamin D_3 moves to the liver and kidneys. These organs **alter** the vitamin D_3. It becomes active vitamin D.*

A. clean
B. change
C. remove

6. What does **fracture** mean in this book?

*Calcium strengthens bone. Without vitamin D, bones can't get enough calcium. They may **fracture** more easily.*

A. break or crack
B. heal or repair
C. aid or help

Answer key on page 32.

Glossary

bacteria
Tiny living things that can either be useful or harmful.

chemicals
Specific kinds of matter. Some chemicals can be harmful, and some can be helpful.

dissolves
Becomes part of a liquid.

immune system
The body system that fights off infections.

ingredient
A food that can be mixed with other foods to make a meal.

nutrients
Substances that living things need to stay strong and healthy.

organic matter
Material that comes from a living thing, such as a plant or animal.

organs
Sets of tissues that have specific jobs in the body.

processed
When a food is changed by adding something to it or preparing it in a certain way.

tissue
A group of similar cells that have a certain job or function.

To Learn More

BOOKS

Gish, Ashley. *Vitamins as Necessary Nutrients.* Minneapolis: Abdo Publishing, 2023.

Golkar, Golriz. *The Digestive System.* Minneapolis: Abdo Publishing, 2023.

Rebman, Nick. *Earth-Friendly Eating.* Mendota Heights, MN: Focus Readers, 2022.

NOTE TO EDUCATORS

Visit **www.focusreaders.com** to find lesson plans, activities, links, and other resources related to this title.

Index

Answer Key: 1. Answers will vary; **2.** Answers will vary; **3.** A; **4.** B; **5.** B; **6.** A